W9-AOX-821

Many thanks to the staff and children at
Redlands Nursery and
The Little Red House Nursery
for their help and advice.

Copyright © 1996 De Agostini Editions Ltd
Illustrations copyright © 1996 Pierre Pratt

All rights reserved.

Edited by Anna McQuinn, designed by Sarah Godwin

First published in the United States in 1996 by
De Agostini Editions Ltd, 919 Third Avenue, New York, NY 10022

Distributed by Stewart, Tabori & Chang,
a division of U.S. Media Holdings, Inc., New York, NY

ISBN 1-899883-47-9
Library in Congress Catalog Card Number: 96-83074

Printed and bound in Italy

Sandra's Sun Hat

Written by
Hannah Roche

Illustrated by
Pierre Pratt

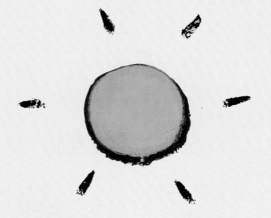

LOOK! It's so sunny
I can see the light
through my curtains.

I'm going to wear
my favorite sun hat.

Camilla, my camel, loves the sun! She can go for days without drinking water. But my flowers need water. When they get too dry, they get droopy.

Su helped me to water my flowers. Then I watered her... so she watered my dog!

We made a big puddle but it dried up really fast.

It's time for lunch.
The kitchen is so cold
my skin gets bumpy!

The park is a great
place to go after lunch.
There are trees, a jungle
gym, a really big pool
and a giant sandbox!

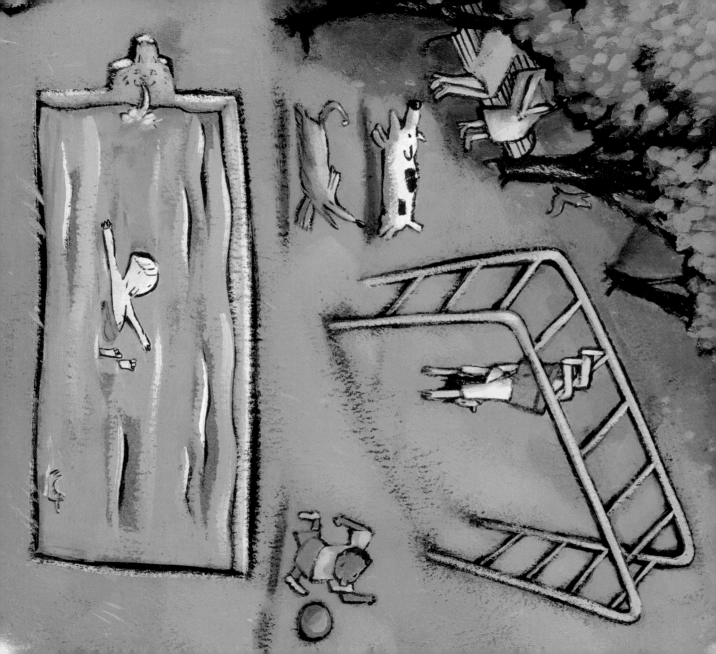

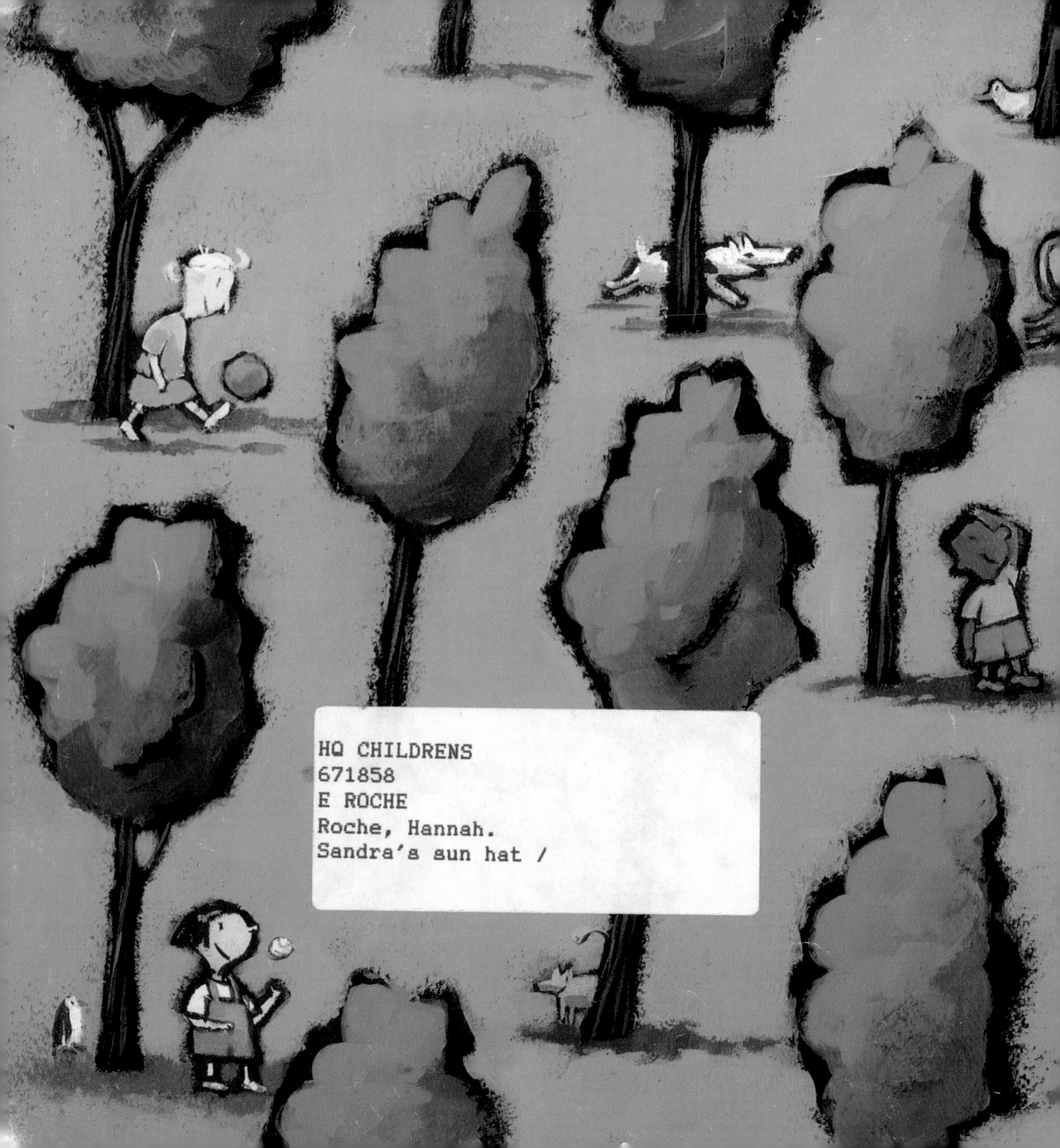